POTENT PROSPECTING

POTENT

PROSPECTING

Curtis W. DeCora

POTENT PROSPECTING

Copyright © 2018 Curtis DeCora
All rights reserved.

ISBN-13: 978-1727883053
ISBN-10: 1727883055

Superior Marketing
PO Box 794
Hayward Wisconsin 54843
www.HaywardMarketing.us

Superior Marketing is a Native American owned Digital Marketing firm specializing in lead generation and outsourced sales solutions. Superior Marketing is a dba and registered and licensed in the state of Wisconsin.

Printed in the United States
First Edition: October 2018
Book design and text composition by Curtis DeCora

POTENT PROSPECTING

POTENT PROSPECTING

DEDICATION

I would like to dedicate this book to a couple of people.

First, my late grandfather, John Bluesky. He was my father figure and showed me the importance of hard work, dedication and commitment. You are gone, but never forgotten.

Second, my children, Kendal and Adel. Daddy loves you and appreciates putting up with my crazy business ideas and many sales meetings throughout the backwoods of Wisconsin and Minnesota.

Lastly, my grandmother, Myrna DeNasha. You've been supportive and helpful for just about everything in my life since I was a child. For that, I appreciate everything you have done.

My colleagues, associates and business partners, you have been pivotal in the growth and development of my 'self' over the last 10 years and I do appreciate your support and will continue to do what I can to support your endeavors.

POTENT PROSPECTING

ABOUT THE AUTHOR

Curtis DeCora is a Native American entrepreneur from the Lac Courte Oreilles Band of Lake Superior Chippewa in Hayward Wisconsin.

After attending Northland College (Ashland Wisconsin) studying business administration while playing collegiate level basketball, Curtis launched into the entrepreneurial octagon in 2009. After 8 years of government contracts, and workforce development sub-contracts, Curtis wanted to focus on small to medium sized business and economic development in tribal communities.

Here, in 2018, Superior Marketing has now served over 163 businesses in 4 countries, and trained 63 sales people throughout the world to become more proficient and productive sales people for their own business and employer.

The primary focus with Superior Marketing is to enhance tribal communities from an economic development standpoint. The primary motivators include job creation, economic sustainability, and diversifying the economic profile for less government dependency.

POTENT PROSPECTING

Don't worry Sales Professionals. This book, is for you.

WHAT OTHERS ARE SAYING ABOUT SUPERIOR MARKETING

"Best freaking business resource EVER! From merchant services, to SEO ranking services, web services, to pep talks no one does it better than Mr. DeCora. I can't possible recommend / refer his services enough. In less than 24 hours of tinkering with our ranking we have received three knew direct reservations, one of which is booking our entire resort! If you're looking to get ahead of the competition and save money on fees give Curtis a call!!!" - Cassidy Wilkozek, General Manager at Musky Joe's Resort

"Truly outside of their class. Curtis went out of his way to help me on multiple occasions. Worth every penny! I highly recommend him and his team to anyone looking to expand their companies client base. - Gilbert Tirado, Forex Trader at iMarkets Live, Inc

"Mr. Curtis gave me some excellent actionable advice on the call we had. He opened up my eyes to the possibilities of prospecting for clients online. Some of which I had no idea of. Thanks for the goldmine of information!"
- Nalin Singh, SEO Consultant

POTENT PROSPECTING

"Superior marketing is genius at what they do, incredible knowledge and experience whenever I talk to them they give me extra every time. I am really happy with the results and will highly recommend them"
- Abu Huraira, Social Media Manager for DevBatch, Inc

"Superior marketing gave me actionable, relevant and extremely valuable ideas I could implement in the same day to improve my sales skills and increase prospects in my business. I am really excited to continue to work with them and see my business grow! Thank you!"
- Jennifer Lee, Technical Consultant

"Gotta give a shootout to the awesome DeCora. This guy is a beast in terms of sales. He knows everything. Also, I was amazed by his charisma and openness to help others. I received tons of great advices from Curtis and he was kind enough to provide me with some free tools regarding lead gen. 10/10."
- Vija Liviu Robert, CEO at Start Small Digital

POTENT PROSPECTING

"Superior Marketing us an excellent organization who can help you accomplish your goals. Next time you'd like to grow, they can help!"
- Nick Dash, Nutritional Consultant at MealCraft

"Very knowledgeable and thorough man. Takes the time that's needed to understand what you need and finds the right tools to get the job done!"
- Darren Landgren, Principal at Landgren Fabrications

"Superior Marketing really helped me out with filling our pipeline to make sure our internal team had leads to follow up with and close. I will keep using them because they offer a great service and value which far exceeds their price."
- Marcelo Bayon, CEO at Sparkki

"One of the best company I have worked with in regards of sales, lead generation, marketing and almost everything. Hit them up for any need related to your business, they got something for everyone."
- Prerak Trivedi, Graphic Designer

"Superior marketing has a solid ground game and excellent customer service" - Aaron Carmody, CEO of Streamline Consulting

POTENT PROSPECTING

TABLE OF CONTENTS

INTRODUCTION	13
SALES CYCLE OVERVIEW	21
RECOMMENDED MINDSET	47
IDEAL CLIENT PROFILE	53
MESSAGING SEQUENCE	65
PROSPECTING TRACKING TOOLS	73
ACTIVITY QUOTA	82
VALUE-CENTRIC RELATIONSHIPS	89
FANATICAL FOLLOW-UP	94
PROSPECTING AND YOU	102
"WHAT ARE YOU DOING"?	111
CHAPTER 12	134
FINAL THOUGHTS	137
THANK YOU	140

CHAPTER 1
INTRODUCTION

POTENT PROSPECTING

POTENT PROSPECTING

INTRODUCTION

Please thoroughly review the sections in their entirety. There are going to be critical elements and viewpoints within this book that enable, encourage and empower you to take action with confidence and consistency.

Professional Bodybuilder, Greg Plitt, quotes, "Anyone can lift weights, do cardio, and eat clean for one day - the truly successful ones are doing it on a daily basis with confidence and consistency.

That's where the truly successful people will reside; at the cross-street of confidence and consistency."

If we apply that quote to the process of prospecting to build a quality pipeline, you must conduct the activities with confidence and consistency.

In the following pages, we will cover the mindset required to proceed with confidence, and process to forge ahead with consistency.

Included in this playbook, you will also find the elements including:

POTENT PROSPECTING

+ Sales Cycle Overview
+ Recommended Mindset
+ Ideal Client Profile
+ Messaging Sequences
+ Prospecting Tracking Tools
+ Recommended Activity Quotas
+ Value-Centric Relationships
+ Potent Prospecting
+ Fanatical Follow Up

The **Sales Cycle Overview** topic includes the very process we have used over the course of the last 10 years in Superior Marketing. The model was taken from a presentation given my Clate Mask in 2001 at a trade show in Chandler, Arizona. This is the very system Infusionsoft uses for their marketing automation software. Pretty neat, don't you think?

Recommended Mindset, to us, is very important, as it drives the entirety of your daily routine, and consistency with fulfilling your . We see books, Life Coaches, and Mindset Coaches all over the internet talking about Millionaire Mindset, and so on. Mindset may be an important factor

POTENT PROSPECTING

in self-development and self-improvement. We cover this in our sections.

Ideal Client Profile is a topic that most clients I consult with, seem to be missing. It is such an important aspect of any sales strategy. It is truly the goal, of who you are going to be contacting as someone who is most likely to do business with you. Why would you focus on that? Well, we do.

Messaging Sequences play a crucial role in ensuring you're uniformly and systematically driving traffic with consistent and predictable results. We'll explore this more in the those sections.

Prospecting Tracking Tools are also an important factor in tracking your progress. The quote by George Santayana states, " you can't know where you're going until you know where you've been"

Activity Quotas have mixed-reviews. The topic alone can divide a room of sales managers and sales trainers, alike. Don't let the word "quota" to fool you. We are focused on activity quotas, not production quotas.

Value-Centric Relationships are focused on relationships lead with a value-laden message or offer. Plain and simple, we'll explore more.

POTENT PROSPECTING

Fanatical Follow Up is where the money is made. I'll show you our process

These are the base topics to help you improve upon your prospecting efforts and use a potent punch of strategies, tactics, and processes to help you fill your pipeline with high quality prospects.

In the following pages, you'll find some of our more granular information on prospecting and the processes we integrate to compile piles of qualified and interested individuals ready to make buying decisions.

There isn't anything sexy or ground-breaking, rather a sequence of sound processes and best-practices to generate a steady flow of consistent and predictable results to fill your sales pipeline.

"Consistent prospecting produces better results than cramming. Daily is best. Daily is better than three call blocks throughout the week. Daily is better than any other strategy you might believe serves you." - Anthony Iannarino

CHAPTER 2
SALES CYCLE OVERVIEW

POTENT PROSPECTING

SALES CYCLE OVERVIEW

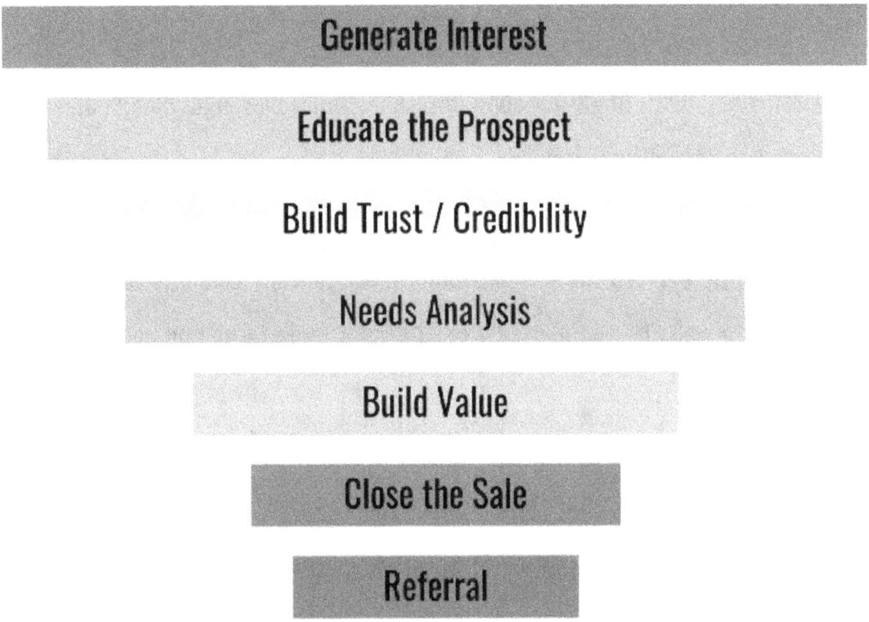

Generate Interest

Educate the Prospect

Build Trust / Credibility

Needs Analysis

Build Value

Close the Sale

Referral

Figure 1: Sales Cycle Overview

The Sales Cycle Overview gives you a visual representation of the process one takes when making a buying decision in regards to any product, service, solution - rather any major life decision.

Consider this for one moment. Think back to the last time you made any type of major buying decision. This can come in the form of new furniture,

POTENT PROSPECTING

vehicle, house, or even someone who is considering dating or marriage.

You go through each one of these steps and stages of the Sales Cycle.

First, you'll need to garner some interest from a message, image, or conversation with a friend.

Second, we explore the related educational content, this can be in the form of a website, social media profile, sales collateral, and consumer reviews.

Third, you consume that content, interview, explore, and discuss to build up your trust and credibility of that product, service or solution.

Fourth, you begin discussing these features, advantages and benefits with the consultant, associate and/or if you're dating, you'll get coffee or lunch with this person to conduct a needs analysis. It isn't a formal analysis, but you'll want to make sure this is a good fit for you and the other party.

Fifth, you'll want to make sure you can see the value in the product, service or solution, as well as a good match for you.

POTENT PROSPECTING

Then, you'll make a decision based on the facts you have at-hand. These facts allowed you to make an informed decision based on the challenges and problems you were experiencing and causing you hard in your life.

Lastly, when the other party delivers and fulfills to meet or exceed your demands - you'll begin to share your story. You become an advocate. You'll tell people who great your realtor is, your car sales consultant, web designer, or plumber.

All of these aforementioned, above, are the classic examples of a solid and sound sales funnel put in place to ensure that you're directing all of your prospects through series of filters, cleaning out those who are not qualified, interested or committed.

When you set up the proper structure of a sales cycle, you'll spit out happy clients who are your best referral sources.

You'll have higher quality clients, and far less refund requests and even less poor reviews.

POTENT PROSPECTING

So, let's get started on helping you put together a high-quality sales cycle.

A. Casting a Wide Net

Create a compelling message that everyone can enjoy and are eager to hear more about. Let me give you an example I have used in the past to cast a wide net.

POTENT PROSPECTING

Figure 2: Buffalo Bay Store

This Facebook Ad, alone produced an opt-in list of 482 people interested in getting more information on promotions, and offers. This Advertisement ran a total of 14 days in the small community of Red Cliff, Wisconsin.

B. Educate the Prospect

Consider the dog that chases the car, for one second. What is to happen if a dog actually catches a car? What will they do with it?

From every corner of the internet, I see Facebook Advertising "Agencies" so focused on running advertisements to generate "leads" for their clients. The fact remains, nobody gets paid until you close a deal.

POTENT PROSPECTING

So, what is next?

We like to explore the notion to educate our prospects once in our sales funnel. Now, that you have them in your grasp - this isn't the time to pepper them with sales pitches, offers, promotions, and so on.

This is the time to educate them on various aspects of your product, services or solutions as it relates to the reason why they signed up in the first place.

EDUCATE

Educate the Prospect.

Focus on their challenge.

Provide Insights.

Help Avoid Landmines

Share Alternatives

POTENT PROSPECTING

These are the essential elements of educating prospects, allowing you to become a trusted advisor and someone who understands the industry and landscape of today's business environment.

Here are 5 ways to educate the prospect:

A. Insights - Information beyond the obvious. Information that isn't presented on brochures or websites. This is insider information you can share with thep prospect.

B. Perspective - Give them a new perspective and new way to look at their current situation. I like to use the analogy of the picture on the wall. You truly never know if the picture on the wall is straight until you take a step back and see it from another person's perspective.

C. Navigate Alternatives - Help your prospects navigate the alternatives on the market today. Why should they choose A, B or C, and it shouldn't be because you make the most money from said deal, but what the prospect will gain from doing business with you.

D. Avoid Minefields - There are always minefields and prospects don't fully understand the full scope of an industry, contract, product, service, or solution. Some buying decisions are just destined to take a turn for the worst, and you can help your prospect avoid minefields.

E. Justify Purchase - We discussed Return-on-Investment, and Total-Cost-of-Ownership, as well as how the solution can impact their revenue, cost reductions, and improvements in efficiency. Price is a myth and should never be a motivating factor in any buying decision.

C. Build Trust and Credibility

The holy grail of sales, "building trust."
How does one accomplish the act of building trust?

As a sales professional, I have worked in various industries, and trained under numerous industry leaders. The fact remains, very few are doing anything to build trust. Every sales professional I have ever worked with or trained under, has pushed, pitched and persuaded. I'm not a fan of bullying prospects into buying decisions.

Prospects and consumers are always on the defense because of this approach, they expect it, they tolerate it, and in short they do what they can to avoid it.

So, how do we build trust and establish credibility? One word. FREE.

POTENT PROSPECTING

Everyone says, "I want to grab 20 minutes do discuss...." or "I'm trying to get 20 minutes of your time to learn more about your business..." and those scream sales pitch for 60 minutes.

Positioning is important and how you frame the offer.

Positioning the free discover call:

Prospecting Script

This is a standard prospecting script you can use in a cold call, knocking on doors or in instant messenger, if you're a digital prospector. Focus on delivery and tonality.

"Mr. prospect, I'm a business strategist and my clients are businesses just like yours, they're service based businesses. My clients increase their sales an average of 23% within the first 90 days of working with me... Mr. Prospect just to be sure I'm not wasting any of your time here today. Let me ask you...

BONUS: 5 Ws for Pre-Qualifying

I'm going to toss everyone a bonus. Here are my 5 Pre-Qualifying questions.

1. What is your biggest challenge?

This isn't anything groundbreaking, but make it relevant to their pre-qualification questions you asked on your initial outreach.

2. Why is that important to you?

Find out why they find these challenges important and why they want to solve them, and now. What makes them get up in the morning and slave hours to solve these challenges, and be that hero.

3. Who is helping you with this?

This is your opportunity to learn who the key playmakers and decision makers involved in this process. Are they leveraging experts, professionals, or one of their employees to handle high-level challenges?

4. Where do you see yourself in the next 3-6-9 months if this challenge persists?

I love this question, because it allows the prospect to paint you a picture of what they foresee will happen if they're unable to solve this problem. Do they close the doors, do they lay off, do they downsize, do they cut back hours of operation, etc? Allow them to paint that picture for you.

5. When can we grab 20 minutes, where I can show you 2-3 ways to solve this challenge?

This is the ask for the Discover Call. In the discovery call, you'll be learning more about their business and offer them free advice on how to solve their challenges. In my hundreds and possibly one-thousand-plus discover calls over the last 3 years, I find that most people struggle with implementation. You can offer them all the free advice in the world, but they still need the process, system and how-to, in order to implement properly.

This does sound like a sales call, and it is, but the intent isn't to sell them anything. The intent is to get their undivided attention in the form of a phone call, Google Hangout, Skype chat, or Facebook Video discussion. I do prefer Google Hangout, because I can share my screen to give them real examples of how my clients are getting the results they desire.

POTENT PROSPECTING

You want to use the answers from the pre-qualifying questions to craft a 2-3 step solution to help them solve their biggest challenge.

Again, give it away for free on that 20 minute call.

Next Step -- ask to conduct a free analysis and send them a brief analysis of their current challenges and how to solve them. This is also called a Needs Analysis.

D. Needs Analysis

Now that you have their biggest challenge, why it is important to them, who the key players are, and where they see their business in the next year if the challenge persists. You also offered the prospect free advice on how to solve their biggest challenge.

You will want to ask them to report back in one week to discuss the results, accomplishments, challenges and failures.

The goal here is to identify if this is a strategy issue or a skill issue. Do they need training, or do they simply need a system and structure?

POTENT PROSPECTING

After that one-week of time, you'll have their 5 Ws answered and their feedback from your advice. Use that advice to offer them a Needs Analysis. This is a simple analysis of their current challenges, and how to solve them based on feedback from their trial period of following your advice.

There are two things that will happen here.

1. Follow + Success + Buy-in:
The prospect will follow your advice to the "T", see some success and then be a raving fan wanting to do business with you, as they see an immediate return-on-investment with just a 20 minute call.

2. Don't Follow + Fail + Spread Rumors:
The prospect, in this case, will not follow the steps, or maybe they do but modify them to meet their comfort levels. After failing, they'll continue to say "it won't work" when others around them are making it happen, then proceed to say you couldn't help them and attempt to discredit your expertise.

POTENT PROSPECTING

The best part, both are absolutely fine. Keep in mind, your job isn't to make everyone happy, it is to find those who are the best fit for you and your business, organize them and conduct business with them.

Let's take scenario 1, where the prospect follows through with your advice, sees results and is ready to move to the next step.

Develop a Needs Analysis which includes your products, services or solutions.

The Needs Analysis will set the stage for a presentation and demonstration.

E. Build Value

Using your findings from the 5 Ws, your results from advice, and the Needs Analysis, now you have the fuel necessary to conduct a proper and thorough value-centric presentation.

The focus, here, is to use 5 Steps to frame the conversation and presentation.

POTENT PROSPECTING

1. <u>State Intention</u>:   I'm going to show you a 10 minute presentation, discuss some of the challenges you're experiencing and if it makes sense - I'm going to be asking for your business. Sound Fair?

2. <u>Gauge Knowledge</u>:   Why don't you take a few minutes and tell me what you know about (your services). Fill the *VALUE GAP* with Insights (information beyond obvious and proceed)

3. <u>Presentation</u>:   Right now, it looks like you're doing (share their current process to get validation and accuracy), is that correct? I recommend we do this, and here's why *PRESENT*

4. <u>Heat Check</u>:   Based on what you saw here today, what kind of questions do you have for me? Address questions *TIE DOWN*, and proceed for close of deal.

5. <u>Ask for the Deal</u>:   It looks like we are a great fit, and have what you need to address your current challenges. I'm going to send you a quick one-page agreement - what is the best email address?

POTENT PROSPECTING

F. Closing the Deal

Closing the deal can seem like a daunting task, however, if you position the presentation and sequence properly, it becomes a natural progression.

Ask for the deal, and recap the entirety of the deal, pricing, terms, conditions, responsibilities, and any other relevant information so you have a transparent posture with no hidden or withheld conditions.

In the example above, I mention an email address, that's for my clients I present to over Google Hangouts. While on the presentation, I send the a DocuSign, and we review the one-page service agreement with all critical information. They simply have to open, click a few buttons and we're done. I send a payment request while on the Google Hangout session and ensure there are no reasons they'll back out of the deal.

There are a couple of reasons for this.

How many times have you presented and gained a verbal commitment, only to have the prospect ghost on you?

POTENT PROSPECTING

This process ties down all objections, raises objections, addresses objections, and walks them right into a buying decision while removing buyer's remorse.

Now. We closed a deal, delivered and fulfilled. Let's get some referrals.

G. Generating Referrals

The process itself is a loose guideline for how to operate within the parameters of a solid sales cycle producing both consistent and predictable pipeline, month-in and month-out. Your sales managers will also appreciate this approach.

Ask for the referral.

"Mr./Mrs. Prospect, so you've been on the product, service or solution for 30 days now. Do you have any concerns I haven't been able to address, yet? "

If the answer is YES. Address those quick and get them solved immediately.

POTENT PROSPECTING

If the answer is NO. Ask for 5 names of someone who would like to get the same level of service as they have received.

"That's great! I'm glad I could be of service to you. Before I go, I would like to ask. Can you give me 5 names of people you know of that could benefit from doing business with me? "

Collect your names, and go out and get some more accounts.

Fun Fact*: The average sales person spends 79% of their time prospecting to generate quality pipeline?*
Referrals cut out 66% of that time, leaving you with 13% to sell and close

CHAPTER 3
RECOMMENDED MINDSET

POTENT PROSPECTING

POTENT PROSPECTING

RECOMMENDED MINDSET

Consider for a minute, the deck of cards.

This deck of cards has 52 cards, and is comprised of four (4) suits.

Those suits are:

+ Hearts → Ready to buy, pre-sold

+ Diamonds → Need more information, research and due diligence

+ Spades → Tire kickers and time wasters

+ Clubs → Remove from list and not interested

The proper prospecting mindset should go as follows.

Every suit, is a prospect category. Most VAs, SDRs, Sales Reps, or Entrepreneurs struggle with prospecting simply because they fear rejection.

Rejection can be crushing and discouraging, on many levels. Instead of pitching and persuading, we want to shift our mindset to (a) educating and (b) engaging.

Let's look at the suits and how we use them to shift our mindset.

POTENT PROSPECTING

Hearts, are ready to buy. They are pre-sold on your product, services, and solutions. You simply need to write them up, or reiterate what they've already confirmed.

The Diamonds require just a little more work. This will be the majority of your qualified prospects   As far as Spaces and Clubs. I highly recommend to simply drop their information into a email drip sequence and push them content.

The goal with prospects isn't to force anything to happen.

 Ready to buy, pre-sold

 Need more information (educational materials)

 Tire Kickers / Time Wasters

 Remove me from your list / Not Interested

Rather, simply sort.

POTENT PROSPECTING

Sort out the prospects as they are presented to you. If they want more information, an email, for example.

"Great! I can definitely send you an email. What kind of information are you looking for? In order to help me get you the more relevant information - let me ask you a few questions....[Insert 5 Ws]"

Keep in mind, the 5 Ws are used to help you pre-qualify your prospects to ensure they are going to be a good fit.

The higher quality clients pay more for you to solve their challenges, as well as provide you with in-depth information to give you a clearer picture of a solution to draft up.

Your focus in prospecting is to find the Hearts and Diamonds, organize them, sort out their challenges, and address them head on with highly engaging conversations.

Quality prospects will share their information with you as far as challenges, team members, past experiences with XYZ, and what their goals are with hopes you can help them achieve their goals.

POTENT PROSPECTING

In conclusion, your job as a sales professional isn't to turn a spade into a heart, but rather to sort out prospects as they come to you, engage them in the process so you may educate them on your products, services and solutions - then aim to build trust and establish credibility.

CHAPTER 4
IDEAL CLIENT PROFILE

POTENT PROSPECTING

IDEAL CLIENT PROFILE

The Ideal Client Profile is pretty basic and straightforward but very crucial in ensuring you have an efficient sales process.

Your Ideal Client Profile is someone we want to retain as a client.

This can prove extremely useful is finding clients who will pay you every month for solving their business challenges.

In determining the ICP (not Insane Clown Posse), we want to look at a couple of variables:

➢ Company
➢ Position
➢ Title
➢ Buyer Type (M-U-T-E)

POTENT PROSPECTING

- Age Range (Millenial or Old School)
- Hands on or Hands off (Outsourcing or Performing Tasks)
- Industry with common challenges you can solve
- Common vertical or niche you serve

These are pretty standard for determining Ideal Client Profile. Once you determine which attributes your Ideal Client or Target Audience will fit, you'll find a much better fit and progression through the sales cycle.

This also helps with targeting and pulling lists to ensure you're reaching out the right prospects.

Let's dive into the ICPs characteristics a little more in-depth.

Company

The company your ideal client works for will be a determining factor for obvious reasons.

If you sell software to health care companies, you're not going to reach out to a fast food chain.

POTENT PROSPECTING

So, now that we go that out of the way.

The company should be included in your list building focus. If they're a health care company, what kind of health care company?

Are they a non-profit, educational health care, direct service provider, intake center, inpatient, or outpatient provider. Their needs will vary greatly as far as a software platform and the data extracted from the platform.

Position

This is another factor, identifying which positions in the hierarchy are standard decision making individuals. Sales research studies show, there are an average of 6 decision makers within any given company. Scout out all executive positions.

Title

Title is sometime assumptive, however, as of the last 3 years, most companies are aiming to become more progressive with their titles.

Some of the most popular titles I have ran across for 2017 and 2018 were "Rockstar", "Ninja" and "Guru." Yes, you read that correctly.

POTENT PROSPECTING

You'll find titles that are task specific, process specific, or organizationally specific. Let me illustrate.

<u>(Task Specific)</u>
Darren Anthony, SEO Guru Manager
Minnesota SEO Gurus

<u>(Process Specific)</u>
Anny Whitehall, Relationships
Midwest Payment Professionals

The standard titles we see organizationally specific include:
Chief Executive Officer, Chief Operations Officer, Chief Financial Officer, Office Manager, Staff Accountant, Accounts Receivable, and so on. These are organizationally specific titles.

Buyer Type

Now, this is what you really want to learn more about. Well, without further adieu, here are the four buying types.

<u>Management Buyer:</u> These folks are typically looking for the best in class, what are the competitors using, is this the best on the market, and how will this position us to our competitors? We are looking at a

POTENT PROSPECTING

high-level plan with out the overall picture. They want their 30,000 foot view. Management buyers only focus on three things; (1) Increase Revenue (2) Decrease Expenses and (3) Expand Market Share or Improve Efficiency.

<u>User Buyer</u>:   The key decision maker in the buying process are the user buyers. Users want to know one thing, "Is this better, and how is it better?" They want to know long it will take to learn, train, and ramp up without losing the integrity of their work quality. It is all about making their life easier, and making things more efficient in their day-to-day operations.

<u>Technical Buyer</u>:   The technical buyer is concerned about the technical aspects with compatibility, what are upgrades like, is it going to crash, does it have the ability to integrate with other parts of their daily processes. We look at business continuity, up-time, maintenance, and most importantly, where will this be in the next 3-5 years? Doe we have to upgrade in 2 years, 3 years, 5 years, or 10 years, or never?

<u>Economic Buyer</u>:   They want to know about one thing. Price. An economic buyer is more concerned about value, and if they're getting a

fair price for their commitment. We are looking at exploring the return-on-investment, total cost of ownership, and break-even point. Economic buyers are more concerned about cost, not price. They want to know what the price of the solution is going to be, as well as down time for installation, training, ramp up time, upgrades, and all costs associated with those steps.

There are numerous deciding factors associated with each buying types, and if you can pinpoint and identify which aspects to discuss while inspiring a buying decision.

Age Range

This one isn't much of a factor, however, the type of outreach best suited to reach this individual will play a role.

While we have younger entrepreneurs, the best method of contact is through social media. Friend requests, commenting on posts, and direct messaging in social platforms are the most direct and fastest methods to get a response.

Older generations prefer a phone call, introductory letter, or to meet up for coffee. I have found that most folks in the older generations, really appreciate you taking the time to pick up the phone, meet in person, or grab a cup of coffee or lunch.

Hands On or Hands Off

Is the ideal client you strive to contact a hands on person, or hands off person? Are they a decision maker who plays a role in the decision making process for others in the organization? This would look like, "We are getting a new point-of-sale system, and you'll have to get with the (first name) to get trained in, it will help us with XYZ" as they're an actual user.

Are they a decision maker that simply states, "Well, Ask (first name) if that would fit her user requirements, as she is the person who handles those aspects."

This is very important when building out your ideal client profile, to improve your understanding and comprehension of the journey the buyer will take, and you can predict those behaviors.

Industry

Industry is important, as it is a wise decision to look at your data. Which industry do you service the best with the most common challenges. Let's say 71% of your clients are dental clinics and the're using your software and client management system. This is an industry you would focus on, or "niche down" on, so to speak. You are specializing in solving challenges for individuals and businesses in this specific industry.

Verticals and Niches

Verticals and Niches are very important when identifying which segment serves as your ideal client. This becomes more granular when you start diving into verticals and niches.

Let me give you an example.

Let's say you have a vending machine, or let's take it a step further. Let's say you have a series of vending machines, product variety presented in such a way that it represents a viable option for health options during lunch and perhaps snacks.
You may want to focus on those who eat lunch and want healthy options. This audience is going to be very large. Let's narrow it down even further

POTENT PROSPECTING

to help give us a boiled down version of an ideal client. We want this as specific as possible.

Let's say we want to focus on those who eat lunch, want healthy options, work in a fast paced environment where a lunch break isn't possible - and - are unable to leave to grab lunch due to time constraints. Now, we have a narrower vision of where our ideal clients are living, working and playing.

This type of exercise allows us to boil down 2-3 ideal target clients. Off hand, we could assume car dealerships, co-working spaces, and construction work zones. We can boil that down even further. Let's say we want to target those who are active at these businesses, those who have food allergies, and those on special diets.

As you can see with the process, the more filters you add, the small and more narrow your audience becomes.

That is the goal with developing Ideal Client Profiles.

POTENT PROSPECTING

You want them to be very specific, narrowing down your audience, allowing you to target prospects based on a specific challenge all of them possess at this moment in time.

CHAPTER 5
MESSAGING SEQUENCE

POTENT PROSPECTING

MESSAGING SEQUENCE

In a perfect world, a messaging sequence that caters to your sales process is what produces the highest quality of results.

I'm going to outline the messaging sequence we have used over the last 10 years to produce the highest quality form of prospects, leads and clients.

The ideal messaging sequence will do a couple of things,
(a) Engage
(b) Educate,
(c) Build Trust and
(d) Establish Credibility.

Here is our version of the Ideal Messaging Sequence.

POTENT PROSPECTING

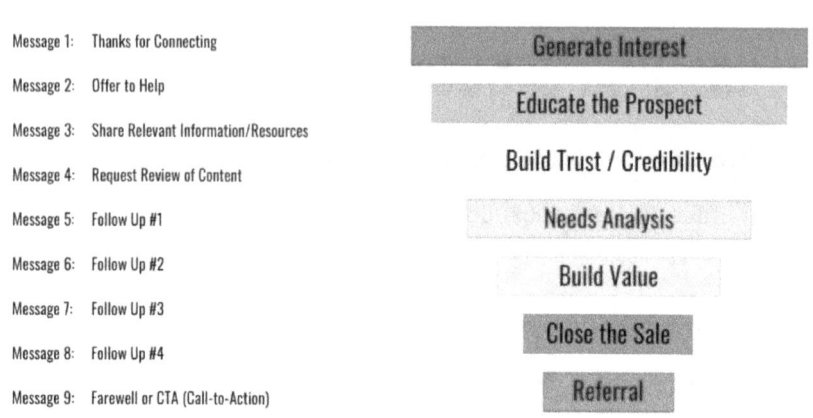

Message 1:	Thanks for Connecting
Message 2:	Offer to Help
Message 3:	Share Relevant Information/Resources
Message 4:	Request Review of Content
Message 5:	Follow Up #1
Message 6:	Follow Up #2
Message 7:	Follow Up #3
Message 8:	Follow Up #4
Message 9:	Farewell or CTA (Call-to-Action)

Generate Interest
Educate the Prospect
Build Trust / Credibility
Needs Analysis
Build Value
Close the Sale
Referral

Figure 3: Ideal Messaging Sequence

In the pages to come, we'll be going over the messaging sequences and which role they play in moving prospects from tire kickers to paying customers.

Message 1: Thanks for Connecting

This is the initial message we include to thank the individual for accepting your connection request. There isn't anything salesy, here. We are simply thanking for them connecting.

Message 2: Offer to Help

Lead with value, always lead with value.. We simply ask that they share some information about what they do, in exchange for some information

POTENT PROSPECTING

about what you do. Once we have permission - we achieved the goal of engagement.

Message 3: Share Relevant Information/Resources

This message now allows you to share information that is important to them and is relevant to their current business challenge. They must have requested a specific topic to engage in - we achieved education.

Message 4: Request a Review of Content

Now that we have shared information, we want to request some time to discuss those educational materials. If they need more information, offer them another resources - we achieve trust and credibility.

Message 5: Follow Up #1

Now, we are in the process of Fanatical Follow Up. We follow up to inquire about their findings and how it relates to their current challenges.

Message 6: Follow Up #2

Once completed, we move on to inquire about why these challenges are important to them and which aspects of their business is most impacted.

POTENT PROSPECTING

Message 7: Follow Up #3

Once completed, inquire about where they stand on the current challenge. Do they plan to automate, delegate or eliminate certain tasks to improve upon these challenges - needs analysis.

Now, we start segmenting out our prospects with a sequence focused on
+ Qualifying
+ Disqualifying

Message 8: Follow Up #4a ******PRE-QUALIFIED and INTERESTED*******

Once completed and identified, we inquire about their plans to automate and requesting a discovery call to learn more about the current situation and determining proper fit.

Message 8: Follow Up #4b *****PRE-QUALIFIED and INTERESTED*******

Once completed and identified, we inquire about their plans to delegate and requesting a discovery call to learn more about the current situation and determining proper fit.

Message 8: Follow Up #4c *******UNQUALIFIED********

Once completed and identified, we commend them for their ability to spot tasks that are either redundant or monotonous and are simply looking to eliminate. There are little to no opportunities here that you can either solve or fulfill.

Message 9: Follow Up #5
If they're not looking to automate or delegate through outsourced means, simply thank them for their time and move on.

This is the process of earning small commitments from the prospect through the messaging sequence and moving them from one mode of thinking and platform to the next.

This is just a sample of a messaging sequence. You are more than welcome to use the template we have provided, but

CHAPTER 6
PROSPECTING TRACKING TOOLS

POTENT PROSPECTING

PROSPECTING TRACKING TOOLS

The only way to improve upon your activities is to track what you're doing.

If you want to run a faster mile, you must track your activity to ensure that you're improving upon your previous effort, run or workout.

In terms of filling your sales pipeline with potent prospecting, you'll want to ensure you're hitting prospects on all levels, from multiple angles to ensure you're in the front of their mind.

Have you heard the term, "out of sight, out of mind?"

Let me illustrate this with an example. When was the last time you had a chat with someone on Facebook, over the phone, or at a networking event where the conversation was great, they seemed interested and wanted to know more.

You follow up with them 2 weeks later, and they give you the, "I'm sorry, but, who are you? We spoke? I'm sorry… I don't recall, what was the topic regarding?"

POTENT PROSPECTING

This is a case of "out of sight, out of mind." In order to break that cycle and utilize pattern interrupt, we must utilize a potent prospecting methodology.

Now, onto tracking. You can use the various tools on the market right now to keep track of all prospect data, you can use:

+ CRM (Customer Relationships Management) Software
+ Email Marketing Software
+ Facebook
+ LinkedIn
+ Excel Spreadsheet
+ Google Sheets

Below is an example of a tracking sheet in Google Sheets, that outline the tasks completed per prospect, and which ones ended up accepting a CTA (Call-to-Action) in the form of a Discovery Call or Needs Analysis.

In this example, we approached 20 ideal clients within our target audience, and ran them through the message sequence.

Out of those 20, 5 completed the entire process and accepted the invitation to a discovery call or needs analysis. The beauty of this process - they are now engaged, educated, trust your word and see you as a credible authority figure.

First	Last	Title	Phone	Email	Connect	Offer	Share	Review	Follow1	Follow2	Follow3	Follow4	CTA
Bob	White	VP of Sales	123-456-7890	bob@whiteconstruction.com	x	x	x	x	x	x	x	x	x
Bob	White	VP of Sales	123-456-7891	bob@whiteconstruction.com	x	x	x	x					x
Bob	White	VP of Sales	123-456-7892	bob@whiteconstruction.com	x	x	x	x	x	x	x		x
Bob	White	VP of Sales	123-456-7893	bob@whiteconstruction.com	x	x							x
Bob	White	VP of Sales	123-456-7894	bob@whiteconstruction.com	x	x	x	x	x	x			x
Bob	White	VP of Sales	123-456-7895	bob@whiteconstruction.com	x	x	x	x	x				x
Bob	White	VP of Sales	123-456-7896	bob@whiteconstruction.com	x	x							x
Bob	White	VP of Sales	123-456-7897	bob@whiteconstruction.com	x	x							x
Bob	White	VP of Sales	123-456-7898	bob@whiteconstruction.com	x	x	x	x	x	x	x	x	x
Bob	White	VP of Sales	123-456-7899	bob@whiteconstruction.com	x	x							x
Bob	White	VP of Sales	123-456-7900	bob@whiteconstruction.com	x	x	x	x	x				x
Bob	White	VP of Sales	123-456-7901	bob@whiteconstruction.com	x	x							x
Bob	White	VP of Sales	123-456-7902	bob@whiteconstruction.com	x	x							x
Bob	White	VP of Sales	123-456-7903	bob@whiteconstruction.com	x	x	x	x	x	x	x		x
Bob	White	VP of Sales	123-456-7904	bob@whiteconstruction.com	x	x	x	x					x
Bob	White	VP of Sales	123-456-7905	bob@whiteconstruction.com	x	x	x	x					x
Bob	White	VP of Sales	123-456-7906	bob@whiteconstruction.com	x	x	x	x	x	x			x
Bob	White	VP of Sales	123-456-7907	bob@whiteconstruction.com	x	x							x
Bob	White	VP of Sales	123-456-7908	bob@whiteconstruction.com	x	x	x	x	x	x	x	x	x
Bob	White	VP of Sales	123-456-7909	bob@whiteconstruction.com	x	x	x	x					x
Bob	White	VP of Sales	123-456-7910	bob@whiteconstruction.com	x	x							x
Bob	White	VP of Sales	123-456-7911	bob@whiteconstruction.com	x	x	x	x	x	x	x	x	x

Figure 4: Google Sheets Prospecting Tracking Tool

Again, this isn't anything groundbreaking, but provides you with a set of tools that enable you to track your prospects through the process without paying for high priced CRM systems that provide the same level of data.

Our team uploads comments as notes, and we can track as a team on one sheet, the entire process of every single prospect.

POTENT PROSPECTING

Without skipping a beat, another team member can pick up where the last team member left off, and continue with the messaging sequence.

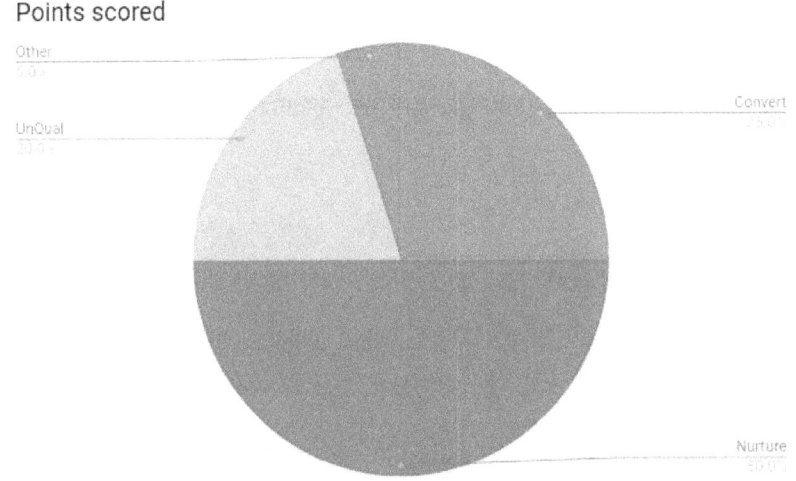

Figure 5: Dashboard of Campaign Performance

In this specific campaign, while highly targeted to resorts in Hayward, Wisconsin, we were able to convert 25% of our prospects to clients through a proper messaging sequence focused on engagement, education, and building trust prior to even discussing pricing, benefits and features.

POTENT PROSPECTING

50% remained in the nurture process where another 3 clients converted.

20% were unqualified after further due diligence into their business and operations.

5% simply didn't engage enough, and have been moved to the drip sequence.

Keep in mind, none of this included paid advertising, this was all direct cold outreach from email, phone calls, and social media messages.

The prospects that do not complete the full sequence, or are DISQUALIFIED, end up in my drip sequence email campaign.

Below is an example of 88 prospects, 23 are opening the emails (28.75%) and haven't removed themselves and continue to consume content on a weekly basis.

I also do this for Landscapers, Lawn Care companies, Hair Salons, Attorneys and Auto Repair companies, in addition to Resorts.

POTENT PROSPECTING

All of my tools are absolutely 100% free, and track all of the data I need to ensure a prospect is never forgotten and continually hit from multiple angles.

I hope that helps you better understand a workflow for tracking prospecting activities, and which category the prospect fits, as well as which
platform and software they should be moved.

Resorts-Hayward2 Regular • Resorts - Hayward Wisconsin	44 Subscribers	30.2% Opens	0.0% Clicks
Resorts - Hayward1 Regular • Resorts - Hayward Wisconsin	44 Subscribers	23.3% Opens	0.0% Clicks

<u>Figure 6: MailChimp Email Drip Sequence</u>

This is a weekly email that goes out to continually educate the prospects on current businesses seeing success with our services, as well as tips and pointers to improve their digital marketing effectiveness.

The resort owners are reading the emails, and MailChimp's heat map function allows me to see which sections they are reading the most, and

POTENT PROSPECTING

they are the PRO TIPS section of my emails, in addition to the number of times they open the email.

CHAPTER 7
ACTIVITY QUOTA

POTENT PROSPECTING

POTENT PROSPECTING

ACTIVITY QUOTA

First, we want to make sure your SDRs, VAs or reps are truly using their time wisely, and maintaining a high level of activity as well as following your sequence which helps in keeping the integrity and quality of the outreach high.

Let's dive in.

SDRs (Sales Development Rep) can complete 25 activities per hour minimum.

Methodology

There are three primary methods for prospecting, you can explore one, or all of them.

Triples ⇒ Your team can hit a minimum of 15 calls, voicemails and emails per hour. You may use this method as a more potent punch per contact, whereas the other methods are a potent daily attack. This

POTENT PROSPECTING

strategy allows you to pack a potent and powerful outreach punch. There are no worries about, "out of sight, out of mind" with this approach.

Daily 100s ⇒ This is a daily discipline I preach, whereas, you take one medium and hit that 100x per day. Example: Monday, you make 100 cold calls. Tuesday, you do 100 emails. Wednesday, you do 100 LinkedIn inMails and Connection Requests, Thursday.... You get the point. This is my favorite approach, as it keeps me consistent in my approach.

Silo Prospecting ⇒ This is a practice done by some of the largest companies, they have a dedicated person to the phones, a dedicated person to LinkedIn, a dedicated person to website inquiries and updates, a dedicated person to Facebook - and so on.

On the next page, I'll show you a diagram of how these work.
Let's look at the various Potent Prospecting Methodologies.

Keep in mind ,these type of methods do allow you to dedicate individuals to outreach activities, track their activity per VA/SDR, or track them based on targeted prospect lists.

POTENT PROSPECTING

This is 100% up to you, on how you want to structure your outreach campaigns and leverage your VAs/SDRs.

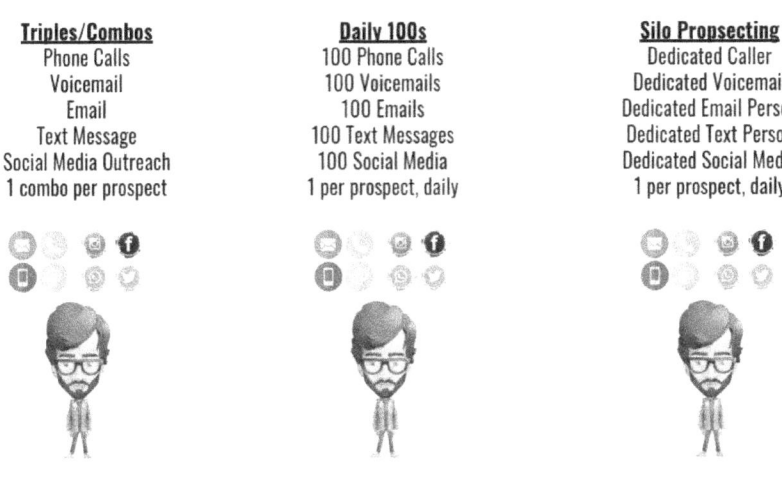

Figure 7: Activity Quota and Methodology

If you're a solopreneur, then you'll want to focus on Combos/Triples or Daily 100s.

If you have a team of dedicated individuals, you can play with the Silo Prospecting method.

CHAPTER 8
VALUE-CENTRIC RELATIONSHIPS

POTENT PROSPECTING

VALUE-CENTRIC RELATIONSHIPS

Circle Research and the Sellinger Group published two studies indicating that today's buyer (Buyer 2.0) has completed 78% of their research prior to reaching out or responding to a sales rep.

This is a metric that illustrates buying confidence. The prospect has completed 78% of their research on their own accord. This comes in the form of visitor your website, your competitor's website, Yelp, Facebook, Google Reviews, as well as your own personal profile.

My philosophy is to get them materials to conduct their research 100% from the resources within your organization. This comes in the form of articles, blog posts, pre-recorded webinars, ebooks, case studies, and other related resources to show your expertise, competence and ethical stance on business related matters.

The other 22% must come from an industry professional - you, so the conversations must go beyond the basic information collected from a Google Search - they are seeking industry metrics, your personal results produced, or average metrics of production from contracting your services. Again, this is identified as, "Insights."

The prospecting can be completely delegated to other team members to ensure you have a human element controlling the quality of content which is shared and directed to the prospect based on their interest with finding a valid solution to meet the demands of their business challenges.

ALWAYS LEAD WITH VALUE

Our aim is to humanize the sales process and ensure that our prospects, clients, and partners will never have to worry about service issues, someone answering the phone, or struggling with business continuity should an issue ever arise.

In reviewing our messaging sequence, which are humanized elements of the process, include offering help. How can I help you? Is there anything I can help you with? Then, we move to engagement which is sharing resources with each party. Send me something about your company, what

POTENT PROSPECTING

makes you unique, what is your greatest accomplishment and why are people eager to do business with you?

Once we achieve engagement, we can now aim to educate with our information.

Our information leads to a discussion reviewing one anothers information (in a perfect world). This isn't a one-size-fits-all formula. This is a framework to allow you to systematize your prospecting to garner higher quality prospects and close more deals with shorter sales cycles.

CHAPTER 9
FANATICAL FOLLOW-UP

POTENT PROSPECTING

FANATICAL FOLLOW-UP

Every high functioning and high performing sales professional will say, "The money is in the follow-up."

I couldn't agree more!

So, we put a ton of time, energy, and resources into finding ways to incorporate more touch-points in our follow-up sequence.

Here is a graphic for you to view, it's ugly, don't get me wrong. However, it is very much a great depiction of what a strong follow-up sequence includes.

POTENT PROSPECTING

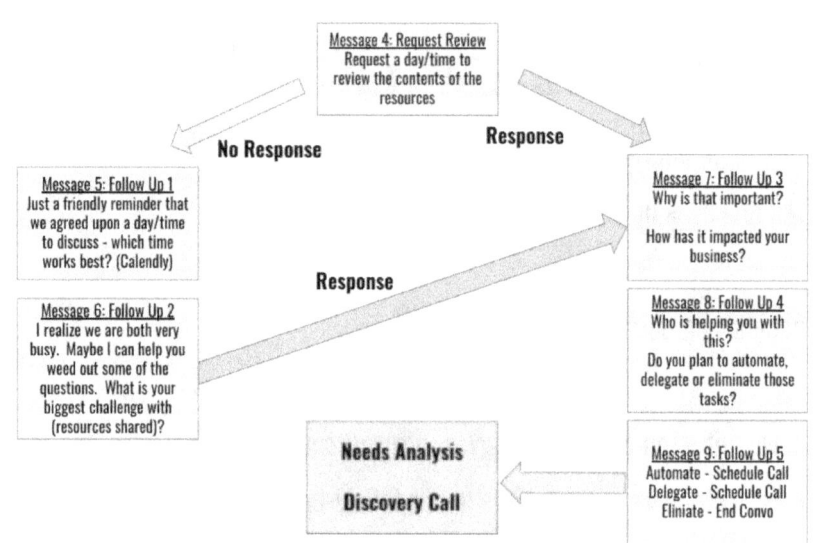

Figure 8: Fanatical Follow-Up Workflow

In our experience, with 10 years of prospecting, outreach, and outsourced sales, the focus has always been on ensuring a proper exhaustion of prospective clients, and messaging sequences.

Let's explore the concept of follow-up.

"TOUCHING BASE"

Why was this ever a follow-up strategy.

POTENT PROSPECTING

"Hey Bob, just touching base. Where are we with XYZ?"

"CHECKING IN"

This is another follow-up strategy I have witnessed from all corners of the sales universe.

Which training program, sales manager or sales director has advocated for this?

"Hey bob, just checking in…"

Now that we have looked at some of the most ridiculous follow-up strategies. Let's review why these are providing negative results.

POTENT PROSPECTING

1. Pesky Sales Person
You come off as a pesky sales person that just wants to talk about features, advantages and benefits, for the sake of your commission check.

2. Nothing of Value
You come off as someone who has nothing to offer; no value to provide.

3. Time Sucker
Per the requirements of your sales manager, or sales director, you're required to have X-amount of conversations and meetings - so you continually suck the time from prospects to satisfy your superiors.

4. Selfish and Prospect Smells It
Your prospect can smell you pushing the highest commissionable products, services, and solutions

5. Inexperienced
Nothing smells like inexperienced more than continually following up with "Touching Base" or "Checking In." It is more than obviously that you

provide zero to not value at all in what you're attempting to offer. It is likely that you have nothing to offer and your inexperience is hanging out.

Here are 3 PRO TIPS to help you make Follow-Up more fruitful

1. Insights

Offer insights, or, information beyond the obvious. They shouldn't be able to find the same article you found and are spewing to your prospect. Give them real-life information based on others in their situation.

2. Continue to Educate

Always, always, provide some form of educational content for the prospect to consume. They should come to you for information, not complaints. The #1 complaint from any business about their service provider, "They never told me." So, address that, and tell them. Plain and simple.

3. Always Lead with Value

Don't worry about the money, just lead with value. "You can have everything in life you want, if you will just help other people get what they want." - Zig Ziglar

In the section ahead, which includes interviews with various entrepreneurs all over the world, I have asked them one question in regards to

POTENT PROSPECTING

prospecting. One of the most common themes are to lead with value, and the sale will follow.

CHAPTER 10
PROSPECTING AND YOU

POTENT PROSPECTING

POTENT PROSPECTING

PROSPECTING AND YOU

Now, I realize that everyone operates in various businesses, industries, and has a variety of buyers from all walks of life.

So, where does one start with developing an effective prospecting strategy?

Do they go to Salesgenie and buy a list that was sold off 100+ times to your competitors?

Do we take that cold call from the sales rep that promises qualified leads from Facebook Ads?

Do we go to Thumbtack?

Do we go to Angie's List?

Those are all questions my clients; current and past have pondered prior to working with us.

POTENT PROSPECTING

The truth is. The choice is yours! However, let me share some information with you on the prospecting front, allowing you a high-impact, and low-cost approach to fill your pipeline with both, qualified and interested prospects to walk through your sales cycle.

In the next pages, we'll cover how to calculate your activity quota to meet and exceed your sales goals. We will cover how to build a targeted list using your Ideal Client Profile, Recommended Mindset, and Scripts. Yes, I'm going to offer you some sample scripts.

Please use the following pages to help craft your best fit for prospecting activities as it relates to filling your pipeline with your ideal clients, based on your industry, market, and sales cycles.
Let's cover the 4 Key Elements to have before you jump into your prospecting activities.

1. Building a List: The list is more important than you may think. While we explore how to build you a list, you may be surprised by the tremendous amount of opportunity you're leaving on the table, as well as missed referrals simply due to lack of process.

POTENT PROSPECTING

<u>Here are the top 10 areas to mine for prospects:</u>
1. Sold customers
2. Servicing customers
3. Lost customers
4. Orphaned customers
5. Unsold customers
6. Vendors
7. Business Partners, and Advisors
8. Referrals
9. Buy list of targeted data
10. Social Media Groups

This isn't an old school memory jogger type of recommendation, rather a list of areas for you to mine which includes potential opportunities you had missed at one point in tie, or another.

We should always be asking for referrals, and connection requests. First are customers. Customers come in all forms. You have your sold customers, your customers you're currently servicing, your customers who were orphaned, and your customers who were unsold (which is technically not a customer). Mine these customers for opportunities. Opportunities, as a customer, you missed in the actual sales cycle. Asking for referral prospects should be part of your process with every single closed-won deal.

Let's take a look at some of the prospecting methods and how to effectively leverage those strategies.

A. Cold Calling

While this isn't the most sexy of the bunch, this does appear to have the most effectiveness in terms of direct contact, and direct response.

I prefer the Grant Cardone method of cold calling. So, here is the Grant Cardone cold calling script you can modify to make your very own.

1. <u>Greeting</u>: Use your name, and only your name. You don't want to get into your company, the history of the company or features, advantages or benefits.
2. <u>Big Claim</u>: Make a big claim associated with using your services, this could be 23% increase in sales, 10 more appointments per month, 50% lower energy bills, or whatever unique value proposition you and your business can back with historical data, case studies, and reviews.
3. <u>Reason</u>: State the reason for the call. This can be something as simple as, "Bob wanted me to give you call, we just helped him....(fill in the

POTENT PROSPECTING

blank)..." or "I noticed an article", or social media post, something along those lines that associates a valid reason to be making and taking this call.

4. <u>Pre-Qualify</u>: This where the 5 Ws come in handy. Use them.
5. <u>Appointment</u>: Book the appointment for the in-depth discussion.

In the last 10 years of conducting business through cold calling, has proved the most effective and fruitful script, to date.

There is no dancing around, 60 minute call, or wasting anyone's time. This is purely about identifying key data points which determine them as an ideal candidate for your product, service, and solution as it relates to their current challenges.

BONUS: In Step 5, "Appointment", I do like to add in the line which includes: "(First Name), what I would like to do is send you over some resources to review leading up to our phone call, video chat, or on-site appointment. What is the best email to get you these resources?"

Personally, I find this more effective because I get an opportunity to find out which area they want to learn more about. This could be prospecting, digital marketing, lead generation strategies, local marketing, or any other e-books, pdfs, or video resources I can share with the prospect to bring them up to speed prior to our meeting.

POTENT PROSPECTING

The primary reason for this. The prospect is going to research anyway, so why not allow them to research my materials from top-to-bottom prior to our meeting, allowing them to bring questions, comments and/or needs for clarification to our appointment.

What I find, is that most prospects bring 3-4 questions with them in regards to my resources, and these are initial talking points for us to start our discussion.

CHAPTER 11
"WHAT ARE YOU DOING?"

POTENT PROSPECTING

"WHAT ARE YOU DOING"?

I took to the streets to find out what my colleagues, partners, and associates were doing to prospect.

Here are their responses.

I asked the question:

"What is your most effective prospecting method and why?"

I, then, asked the follow up question:

"How has this method impacted your closing ratio?"

The answers will surprise you and the common theme is exactly what we discuss in this book.

POTENT PROSPECTING

You will find a lot of the entrepreneurs find the best results when focused on leading with value, developing a relationships, building trust and establishing credibility.

Let's dive in, and get acquainted with some entrepreneurs from all over the world who are finding great successes with prospecting, and which platforms they find best to reach their target audience.

POTENT PROSPECTING

ENTREPRENEUR: Sabrina Santoro

Name: Sabrina Santoro
Title: CEO
Company: Santoro Solutions
Location: Dallas, Texas
Industry: Digital Marketing and Consulting

What is your most effective prospecting method, and why?

My most effective prospecting method would probably have to be utilizing Facebook groups. When people post about topics that I know I can help them with I can reach out to them in a friendly way. Then ultimately take the conversation to private message and exchange numbers. We can hop on a call and see if my product or service is a good fit for them!

How has this method impacted your closing ratio?

Closing ratio is high - because the people are not completely "cold". They have already expressed something that they need help with! The hardest

POTENT PROSPECTING

part would be volume and staying organized to not let anyone fall through the cracks.

POTENT PROSPECTING

ENTREPRENEUR: Vija Liviu Robert

Name: Vija Liviu Robert
Title: Digital Consultant
Company: Start Small Digital
Location: Bucharest, Romania
Industry: Website Design and SEO
URL: www.StartSmallDigital.com

What is your most effective prospecting method, and why?

I keep a close relationship with my clients and they always send people my way. Second best thing. Give tons of value in social media groups.

I also moderate a really big romanian entrepreneurs group and lead with value as much as possible, which affords me opportunities for more discovery calls with interested prospects.

How has this method impacted your closing ratio?

POTENT PROSPECTING

My closing ratio has increased substantially since using the "lead with value" method, most prospects are polarized to the advisor that throws valuable content around like confetti.

POTENT PROSPECTING

ENTREPRENEUR: Brandon Cornelison

Name: Brandon Cornelison
Title: VP of Sales
Company: Praetorian Group
Location: Las Vegas, Nevada
Industry: Executive Security Firm
URL: www.pgglobalsecurity.com

What is your most effective prospecting method, and why?

I like email blast/follow up phone call combo. Its a quick one two punch. You can usually get good results and direct conversations with key decision makers versus messing around with social media and trying to make contact with decision makers who aren't using the these particular platforms.

How has this method impacted your closing ratio?

POTENT PROSPECTING

My closing ratio are high. The only down side of the combo method, is that it is time consuming, and you're limited by your activity and pipeline. However, the sales cycles are much shorter with direct contact.

POTENT PROSPECTING

ENTREPRENEUR: Kenneth Morris

Name: Kenneth Morris
Title: Principal
Company: Morris Consulting LLC
Location: Mansfield, Ohio
Industry: Merchant Services
URL: www.MidwestEPI.com

What is your most effective prospecting method, and why?

I love to get out and meet people face to face. You can talk with them all you want over phone and internet, but nothing beats putting a face to a voice.

How has this method impacted your closing ratio?

As previously mentioned, you can talk with them all you want over email or social media. Nothing beats a good face-to-face discussion, solid hand shake, and first impression like an in-person meeting.

POTENT PROSPECTING

My sales cycles have decreased from about 12 weeks down to 8 weeks, and those that normally take 5 weeks, are down to 2-3 weeks. There are some you can catch at the right moment and close those deals on the spot. You never hear about that with Facebook advertising or email marketing.

POTENT PROSPECTING

ENTREPRENEUR: Bill Somerville

Name: Bill Somerville
Title: Principal / Lead Generation
Company: Dawn Patrol Digital
Location: Briney Breeze, Florida
Industry: Data and Lead Generation
URL: www.dawnpatroldigital.com

What is your most effective prospecting method, and why?

The phone. Not so much Cold Calling. I would say a sales guy that utilizes the phone - checks in on his prospects (on top of his account managers) and actually cares, because that's where I pull my referrals and my most convert-able prospects. Getting started initially it was definitely the relationships I build through cold calling and developing a tight follow up process.

How has this method impacted your closing ratio?

POTENT PROSPECTING

It all starts and ends on the phone. Fom selling commodities, to selling leads, to selling digital marketing, the most conversions and closed accounts will happen over the phone, versus any other form of prospecting ever will.

POTENT PROSPECTING

ENTREPRENEUR: Marcelo Bayon

Name: Marcelo Bayon
Title: Chief Executive Officer
Company: Sparkki
Location: Salt Lake City, Utah
Industry: Online Education/Training
URL: www.sparkki.com

What is your most effective prospecting method, and why?

I grew up in door to door sales so I know if I hop on the phone and start dialing or knocking doors I will get something... Even if its 1-2 leads.

How has this method impacted your closing ratio?

As long as you're targeted in your approach, it's effective. I can get facebook impressions all day but I still need to get better. I have facebook ads running for solar panel installation and nothing bro. Just a sh*t ton of impressions. Closing deals is a person-to-person process, or humanized, as you call it.

POTENT PROSPECTING

ENTREPRENEUR: Gilbert Tirado

Name: Gilbert Tirado

Title: ForEx Trader

Company: iMarkets Live Inc

Location: Avondale, Arizona

Industry: Foreign Currency Exchange

URL: www.iMarketsLive.com/Gilbertst

What is your most effective prospecting method, and why?

Providing value is the best way to prospect. I've found that when im building anything, if I give people information that they didn't have or couldn't get before, that generates interest with my prospects. Then, I use a swiss cheese strategy where I leave holes and they gotta buy the holes. sign ups come in significantly faster than anything else i've used. My advice is to let them come to you rather than you going to them. The most important thing is to put yourself in high traffic areas. which can be anything from building a facebook group of like minded individuals or sitting in the mall and giving out flyers with tidbits. etc.

POTENT PROSPECTING

How has this method impacted your closing ratio?

There is no pitch. At least we know they're consuming our content to make informed decisions - making for higher quality leads.

POTENT PROSPECTING

ENTREPRENEUR: Michael Clarquist

Name: Michael Clarquist
Title: Multimedia Artist
Company: 187 Ink
Location: Hayward, Wisconsin
Industry: Native American Arts
URL: www.morrowsnativeart.net

What is your most effective prospecting method, and why?

Conversing and understanding to adjust to the the current conversation. Asking relevant questions to what I don't understand in the areas they're speaking helps me learn more as well as make the recipients feel adequate or relevant in the conversations. In other words, be involved. Then analyzing what we talk about and answer respectively or in a timely manner to make the meat of the conversation effective to the goals or purpose of the beginning questions or topic that created the conversation. But the whole of what I said earlier is better lol. There is so much more to understanding the mind lol. If we talk about something and roll to examples to specify the meaning or pinpoint the type of definition were

POTENT PROSPECTING

going for also helps because even knowing what a word means also leaves interpretation.

How has this method impacted your closing ratio?

As long as you show you care, there isn't any deal you cannot close.

POTENT PROSPECTING

ENTREPRENEUR: Elisha Isreal

Name: Elisha Isreal
Title: Founder
Company: AI Digital Suite
Location: Eugene, Oregon
Industry: Digital Marketing
URL: www.aidigitalsuite.com

What is your most effective prospecting method, and why?

My favorite prospecting method is content marketing combined with direct
personalized outreach to targeted prospects. Paid traffic is a close follow up for scaling companies. So what does that mean and look like in practice? Nowadays, digital media gives us access to tap into the channels where our most ideal prospects are online. Whether through social media platforms like LinkedIn or Facebook or through search engines, we have the ability to place ourselves exactly in front of our most ideal prospects. One of the best ways to do this is to create content that is both helpful and demonstrates expertise. Since most people don't

POTENT PROSPECTING

implement, this allows you visibility as the expert and you become known as the go to option for what you offer. When you combine this public facing content marketing strategy with direct outreach (social media messages, email, calls) to ideal prospects, what happens is that these prospects now see you as an expert before you ever reach out. The added benefit is that, as you become known as an expert through the content you publish, you have unexpected opportunities from people reaching out to you for your services or through referrals. I'm also a huge advocate for digital advertising, although this is best for companies that are prepared to invest into scaling and have proven systems for sales and fulfillment in place. If those systems are in place, the opportunity to drive targeted traffic towards your ideal sales metric (I.E. appointments) is prolific and well underused in today's market. These kind of systems are scaleable while also having a minimal time investment in relation to finding new prospects, leading to an effective method when factoring in the cost/benefit analysis of consistently pursuing new prospects and the labor involved with that process. I also recommend investing time and energy into Search Engine Optimization so that your ideal prospects can find you when they search for you. This is worth noting earlier and is a stable long term play for any business looking to get targeted traffic and leads without investing heavily into paid traffic. When properly set up and

POTENT PROSPECTING

combined with digital advertising, this combination of search, social and digital advertising leads into a comprehensive digital strategy that can be even further advanced through media features, influencer marketing and strategic partnerships. At the end of the day, the goal is to have targeted conversations with ideal prospects. Identify where they are and go have those conversations. No single strategy is better than the other, whether online or offline. Learn your market, become part of your market, be where they are, speak their language and do your best to lead through service. The rest is a rather straightforward process from there.

POTENT PROSPECTING

ENTREPRENEUR: Curtis DeCora

Name: Curtis DeCora
Title: Principal / Business Strategist
Company: Superior Marketing
Location: Hayward, Wisconsin
Industry: Marketing and Sales
URL: www.HaywardMarketing.us

What is your most effective prospecting method, and why?

As the creator, advocate and practitioner of the Daily 100s, I absolutely recommend the Daily 100s for anyone wanting to produce a more effective prospecting strategy. This includes forms of direct contact to reach all of my ideal clients and target prospects. Phone calls and knocking on doors are the best method for me to get direct answers on meetings, identifying challenges, and assessing needs. I use the digital formats for purposes of follow-up, sharing educational content, or helping them engage in our relationship going forward. It is all about; qualify, qualify, qualify. As long as you're using a qualifying sequence, you'll be just fine. One additional bonus to help me determine qualification standards, is the practice of "Moving Platforms" as I like to call it. I move the prospect from one platform to another as a sign of commitment in the process. If I can move them from a cold call to a video chat on Google Hangouts, that's a small commitment on their part, and can measure that as buy-in from the prospect. I aim for 4 changes of platform, every change represents buy-in. The more changes, the more qualified, and I can measure every single change of platform, and every single aspect of the buyer's journey to score my leads.

How has this method impacted your closing ratio?

This has been an absolute game changer for me since implementation, 4 years ago. This allows me to score leads from start to finish and refine my prospecting process to ensure I'm scoring leads, and moving them through the process properly with highly engaging content. I close at 83% over the last 10 years, and have improved to over 90% this year, alone.

CHAPTER 12
FINAL THOUGHTS

POTENT PROSPECTING

FINAL THOUGHTS

As we wind down this book, I want to leave you with some final thoughts.

First Thought

Don't forget to register for the course, "Potent Prospecting" which is a 4 week crash course in prospecting techniques, mindset, developing your Ideal Client Profile, Activity Tracking and overall, filling your empty sales pipeline.

Register at: www.PotentProspecting.us

Second Thought

Take all of the information you find in this book as a guideline, or frame work if you will. This isn't a cookie cutter approach, or the ultimate method and system for prospecting. I'm simply showing you how we at Superior Marketing have done prospecting over the last 10 years, and why we fell it is the best approach for our ideal client profile. However, the activities recommended will produce results, regardless of your industry, we are simply advocating for high volumes of activity that are both deliberate and targeted.

POTENT PROSPECTING

Third Thought

All of the information provided in this book are the same topics in the Potent Prospecting Course, and all of my prospecting coaching services. We simply breakdown the industry-specific approach to best fit your unique needs, and challenges as it relates to filling your very own sales pipeline with prospects that are both qualified and interested.

Fourth Thought

Prospecting is never just "one-thing" that will make or break your effectiveness and affect your results. Prospecting effectiveness is about the entire process, the culmination of the activities in a sequence that ties together the components of a Potent Prospecting process. We want all of those components to tie in (a) generating interest (b) engaging the prospecting (c) building trust, (d) establishing credibility, and most of all (f) creating a value-centric relationship.

Final Thought

Humanize. The. Sales. Process. I cannot stress this enough. I see more and more individuals from all corners of the internet talking about automating their marketing and sales. While, it is great to have a sales

POTENT PROSPECTING

page that converts and collects card information. You still run the risk of losing potential clients and customers by removing the human element.

Automating the sales process allows you to generate interest, engage the prospect, and convert the sale. Humanizing allows the same exact elements, but includes building trust, establishing credibility, creating a value-centric relationship, and facilitating a buying decision. We often times forget that humans are the motivating factor behind facilitating buying decisions.

Think of your last purchasing decision, whereas someone was able to help you through the buying process with navigating alternatives, avoiding minefields, and calculating ROI or total cost of ownership, as it relates to your purchase. Sales pages just don't do that. Humanize the process, ladies and gentlemen.

THANK YOU

From the bottom of my heart, Thank you so much for investing in my book.

POTENT PROSPECTING

It truly means a lot to have one of the little guys, garner so much love from the publishing of my first book.

Please be sure to let me know if you're ever in need of guidance or support of your very first book, online course, start of a small business, or any other major life-business event.

I'm more than happy to help our a fellow entrepreneur and provide as much support and guidance as my fellow mentors have supplied to me.

From all of us here at Superior Marketing, and from myself and my children, Kendal and Adel.
We thank you!

Curtis DeCora
Principal / Business Strategist
Superior Marketing
PO Box 794 | Hayward WI 54843
www.HaywardMarketing.us